Henry VIII

Moira Butterfield

FRANKLIN WATTS
LONDON·SYDNEY

Designer Jason Billin
Editor Sarah Ridley
Art Director Jonathan Hair
Editor-in-Chief John C. Miles
Picture research Diana Morris

First published in 2006 by Franklin Watts

Copyright © 2006 Franklin Watts

Franklin Watts
338 Euston Road
London NW1 3BH

Franklin Watts Australia
Level 17/207 Kent Street
Sydney NSW 2000

A CIP catalogue record for this book
is available from the British Library.

Dewey classification number: 942.05'2'092

ISBN 978 0 7496 6448 0

Printed in China

Franklin Watts is a division of Hachette Children's Books.

Note to parents and teachers:
Every effort has been made by the Publishers to ensure
that the websites in this book are suitable for children, that
they are of the highest educational value, and that they
contain no inappropriate or offensive material. However,
because of the nature of the Internet, it is impossible to
guarantee that the contents of these sites will not be
altered. We strongly advise that Internet access is
supervised by a responsible adult.

Picture credits
The Royal Collection © 2005 Her Majesty Queen
Elizabeth II: 28

Alister Berg/Alamy: 7
The Berger Collection of the Denver Museum of Art,
USA/Bridgeman Art Library: 6
Jonathan Blair/Corbis: 17
Richard Booth/AKG Images: 8
Cambridge University Library: 9b
Dagli Orti/Civiche Racc d'Arte Pavia/Art Archive: 16
Dagli Orti/Musée Chateau de Versailles/Art Archive: 13
Lara E. Eakins: 27
English Heritage/HIP/Topfoto: 5t, 20
Jarrold Publishing/Art Archive: 15
Erich Lessing/The Louvre, Paris/AKG Images: 22
Magdalen College, Oxford/Bridgeman Art Library: 14
Olivier Martel/Corbis: 18
Palazzo Barberini, Rome/Bridgeman Art Library:
front cover, 1
Graeme Peacock/Alamy: 12
Erik Pelham/National Trust Photo Library: 5b
Philllips/Bonhams, London/Bridgeman Art Library: 4
Private Collection/Bridgeman Art Library: 29t
Private Collection/Christies Images/Bridgeman Art
Library: 19
Roger-Viollet/Topfoto: 11
The Royal Armouries/HIP/Topfoto: 10
Eileen Tweedy/Magdalene College, Cambridge/
Art Archive: 21tr
Walker Art Gallery, Liverpool/Bridgeman Art Library: 26
Watts: 9t, 24
Trustees of the Weston Park Foundation, UK/Bridgeman
Art Library: 23
Reproduced by permission of the Dean and Canons of
Windsor: 29b
Woodmansterne/Topfoto: 25
Adam Woolfit/Corbis: 21bl

*Every attempt has been made to clear copyright. Should
there be any inadvertent omission please apply to the
publisher for rectification.*

Contents

Who was Henry VIII?

Henry VIII was King of England between 1509 and 1547.

A member of the Tudor family, Henry and his relatives ruled England for 118 years. As a result, this period in history is often called the Tudor era. Henry is famous for having a very eventful reign, including six marriages. Many books, plays and films have been based on his life.

The first Tudor

Henry VIII's father, Henry VII, was the first Tudor to rule England. He won the throne by defeating the previous king, Richard III, at the Battle of Bosworth in 1485. The victory brought to an end 30 years of English civil war, called the Wars of the Roses. It was fought between two powerful noble families called the Houses of Lancaster and York. Henry's father was a Lancastrian.

A portrait of Henry VII, who was born in Pembroke Castle, Wales, in 1457.

 Did you know?

Many kings and queens share the same name, so writers usually use Roman numerals to show which one they are referring to. "V" means 5, so "VIII" is 5 + 1 + 1 + 1 = 8.

Key fact

After the Battle of Bosworth, Henry VII took the badge of the Lancastrians, a red rose, and mixed it with a white rose, the badge of the Yorkists. He created a new badge, the Tudor rose, which you can see on Tudor buildings and in paintings of the time.

Henry is born

As soon as Henry VII won the throne he married Elizabeth of York, to end the split between the families of York and Lancaster. She had a daughter and two sons, Arthur and Henry. Her second son, Henry, was born at Greenwich on 28 June 1491.

Peace and wealth

Henry grew up in a country that his father helped make peaceful and wealthy. Most people lived in their own small villages and farmed for a living. Farmers sold their goods in local market towns. Henry himself lived in the royal palaces of London, England's biggest city both then and now.

A view of the interior of the Tudor Merchant's House at Tenby.

Go and visit

In Tudor times, English and Welsh market towns began to grow in size. If you visit one you might see Tudor buildings, such as the Merchant's House in Tenby, Pembrokeshire. Inside you can see how a Tudor town family lived.

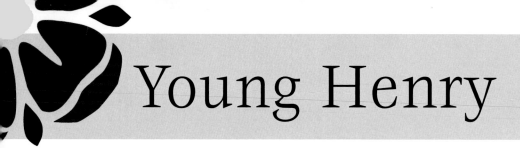

Young Henry

The young Henry did not expect to be king, as he was Henry VII's second son.

His older brother, Prince Arthur, was the heir (the next-in-line) to the throne, but Arthur became ill and died at the age of 16. Overnight Henry, who was only 11, became the new heir.

Henry the scholar

The young Henry was educated so that he could become a powerful priest when he grew up. He learnt theology (religious studies), Latin, Greek, music and poetry. He didn't go to school but was taught by a personal tutor, the court poet John Skelton. He was clever and good at his studies.

His brother's wife

Arthur had been married to Catherine of Aragon, the daughter of the King of Spain. When Arthur died, his father announced that Catherine would marry Henry when he was old enough. Spain was a very powerful nation, and the English king wanted to have a strong alliance (friendship) with them.

A portrait of Henry as a young man.

> ### Did you know?
>
> The death of Prince Arthur was not unusual. Six out of ten children died before adulthood in Tudor times.

Henry the heart-throb

Henry was a very popular prince. He was intelligent, outgoing and handsome. He had red hair and grew to 1.8 metres, very tall for a time when the average height was 1.6 metres.

He loved music, art and poetry and enjoyed sports, such as real tennis – an early form of tennis – which he played particularly well.

 Key fact

Henry was expected to make a career in the Roman Catholic Church, which was very powerful across Europe. The head of the Church was the Pope in Rome.

 Go and visit

Henry played a form of tennis we call "real tennis". You can visit his real tennis court at Hampton Court and see people playing.

"Long live the King"

Henry VII died at the age of 52. His son, Henry, was crowned King of England at Westminster Abbey on 23rd June, 1509. Crowds cheered him, looking forward to a bright new reign.

Go and visit

Henry's grand coronation took place at Westminster Abbey in London (above), which you can still visit today. Nobles and churchmen attended this event.

Henry's coronation was a very grand affair. He was anointed (blessed) by the Archbishop of Canterbury, and all the nobles present had to promise to obey him. The coronation was followed by a big feast. The waiters were led into the banqueting hall by nobles on horseback.

Out with the old

Henry's father was seen as a grumpy money-grabbing ruler, so people were pleased to see Henry on the throne. They thought that he would bring kinder times and lower taxes. Henry increased his popularity by immediately ordering the execution of his father's two most hated tax-collectors, Edmund Dudley and Sir Richard Empson.

A painting of Henry VIII's coronation

A wedding

Shortly before the coronation, Henry married his brother's widow, Catherine of Aragon. Some churchmen thought it was unlawful to marry a brother's widow, but the Pope gave his personal permission. Henry very much wanted to marry Catherine, whom he had known since he was a child. They seemed very happy together.

 Did you know?

Catherine of Aragon was betrothed (promised in marriage) to Henry's brother Arthur. She married Arthur when she was 16, but he died six months later. She had to wait seven years to marry Henry, by which time she was 23. The picture below shows their wedding.

 Key fact

The nobles were the most important families in England. Some of them were related to the royal family. They owned large estates and were wealthy and powerful in their own right.

The golden king

The young King Henry's court was a lively fun-filled place, and he was seen as a good ruler.

Not only was he handsome and athletic but he was clever and a devout Roman Catholic. He invited musicians and artists to his court, furnished his palaces luxuriously and had fine objects made for them.

Henry's court

Wherever Henry went he was surrounded by the court, a group of noblemen and women who had job titles such as "master of the horse" and "lady-in-waiting". It helped Henry to have the most powerful people in the land near to him because at court it was difficult for anyone to plot privately against him and keep it a secret.

Henry's tournament armour at the Royal Armouries in Leeds

 Go and visit

At The Royal Armouries in Leeds you can see tournament armour made for Henry VIII. This type of armour was made for fighting on foot, not jousting. Henry wore it at the Field of the Cloth of Gold (see page 13).

The King at play

Henry was rather bored by government duties and preferred to spend the day doing his favourite hobbies. He loved to hunt in the forests that were attached to his royal palaces, and he flew his own trained birds of prey. Music and dancing were frequent events. Some of the music was written by Henry himself.

Jousting tournaments

Henry loved jousting. The joust was first invented so that knights could practise the skills they might use in a real battle. Henry's tournaments were sporting events rather than battle practice. Even so, jousting was dangerous, and often knights were injured or killed.

Jousting knights were the sports heroes of their day. This painting shows Henry jousting in front of a crowd.

Foreign friends and enemies

In Henry's time Spain, France and the Holy Roman Empire (modern-day Germany) were the strongest European countries. Henry wanted England to equal them and he wanted to be seen as a strong brave military leader, so he went to war.

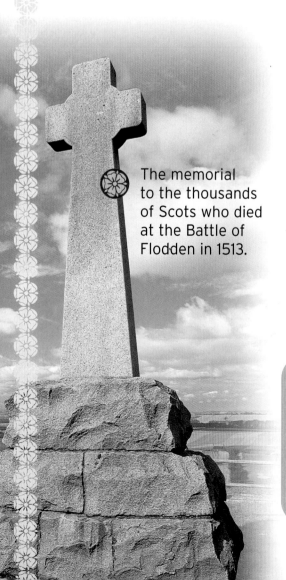

 The memorial to the thousands of Scots who died at the Battle of Flodden in 1513.

Encouraged by his father-in-law, Ferdinand of Spain, Henry campaigned against France in 1512 and 1513. Although the battles ended with English victories, Ferdinand went behind Henry's back and reached secret deals with France to secure land for himself. This angered Henry greatly.

Watch the Scots

While Henry and his army were in France his own brother-in-law, James IV of Scotland, invaded England with support from the French. The Scots were heavily defeated at the Battle of Flodden. Ten thousand Scots were killed, including James himself.

Key fact

Alliances (friendships) between European countries changed regularly during Tudor times. Enemies became friends and friends enemies as every country tried to get as much land and wealth as it could.

Go and visit

At Hampton Court, near London, you can see a painting of the Field of the Cloth of Gold, and one of Henry embarking on a ship to go there. Both paintings hang in a gallery said to be haunted by Catherine Howard, Henry's fifth wife.

Peace and a party

Henry's chief minister, Cardinal Thomas Wolsey, urged the King to make peace with France. So, in 1520 Henry sailed across the Channel with his court and set up camp near Calais to meet with the French King Francis I and discuss peace. There was feasting and music, and 2,800 fine tents for everyone to stay in. The grand glamorous event was called the Field of the Cloth of Gold.

This painting shows Henry VIII arriving at the Field of the Cloth of Gold in France.

Did you know?

At the Field of the Cloth of Gold, fountains were set up to flow with red wine for the length of the meeting – two weeks in all!

Row with Rome

Henry desperately wanted a son to rule after him. Without one, he thought other nobles might try to take the crown once he died.

But Catherine of Aragon, despite several pregnancies, produced only one healthy child, a daughter called Mary. After nearly twenty years of marriage, Henry decided Catherine was getting too old to bear a son. At the same time, he fell in love with another woman, Anne Boleyn.

Divorce or else

Henry wanted to divorce Catherine, and wanted Wolsey to persuade the Pope to "annul" the marriage, which meant to declare it had never existed in the first place. Henry now said that because he had married his brother's widow, the marriage didn't count in law. When the Pope refused, Henry fell out with Wolsey and had him arrested. Wolsey died soon afterwards. Otherwise Henry would probably have had him executed.

 Did you know?

Henry VIII did have a healthy son, called Henry Fitzroy, when he was young. But this baby was born to one of the King's mistresses, not the Queen, so he could not be heir to the throne.

Cardinal Thomas Wolsey

 Key fact

During this time, many people in northern Europe were unhappy with the power and behaviour of the Roman Catholic Church. A German monk called Martin Luther wrote books attacking the Catholic Church. He set up a new branch of Christianity called "Protestantism".

Taking charge

Henry appointed two new ministers, Thomas Cromwell and Sir Thomas More. Thomas Cromwell persuaded Henry to make the Church in England independent of Rome, and for Henry to become the head of the English Church. This plan was achieved by two important new laws: the Act of Appeals (1533) and the Act of Supremacy (1534). Now Henry no longer needed the Pope's permission to divorce.

Agree or die

Many devout Catholics in England were very upset by the break with Rome. One of Henry's chief ministers, Sir Thomas More, refused to recognise Henry as the head of the Church of England. Despite being an old friend of Henry's, he was tried for treason and beheaded in 1535.

Go and visit

Visit Hampton Court, near London, a fine palace built by Wolsey. Henry liked it so much that he made Wolsey give it to him as a present!

Hampton Court Palace

15

Divorce and death

Henry married Anne Boleyn in January 1533, four months before he was officially divorced from his first wife.

Catherine went to live in a convent, and Henry chose not to see his daughter, Mary.

Another daughter

Anne was pregnant when she married Henry and she gave birth to a daughter, Elizabeth, in September 1533. Her second child was a boy, but he was born dead. Henry had so wanted a son that the birth of Elizabeth was a great disappointment to him. Eventually she would become one of England's great monarchs, Elizabeth I.

Guilty!

Henry quickly grew tired of Anne and wanted to get rid of her. He accused her of treason, for having love affairs with other men. She was tried, found guilty and executed in the Tower of London in 1536, three years after marrying Henry.

Another wedding, another death

Henry took a new mistress, Jane Seymour, a noblewoman and one of Anne's ladies-in-waiting. She married him two weeks after Anne's execution.

Key fact

Henry accused Anne Boleyn (above) of being unfaithful but the charges were probably untrue. Torture was used to make her so-called lovers admit to whatever Henry wanted. Torture was often used to get evidence at this time.

A view inside the Tower of London. Tower Green is in the centre.

Henry's son

In 1537, Jane gave birth to a son, Edward, but she died twelve days later. Henry was heart-broken although he did have a son and heir at last. Edward would later become king for a short while after Henry's death, but he himself died when he was only 15.

 Go and visit

Visit the Tower of London, the main prison and place of execution for important prisoners in Tudor times. Anne Boleyn was executed on Tower Green, and the spot is marked with a plaque.

The end of the monasteries

The Roman Catholic Church had many English monasteries and convents, which housed communities of monks or nuns.

After Henry became Head of the English Church, he had them all closed down by his chief minister at the time, Thomas Cromwell.

All about monasteries

Monks spent their days working in the monastery or praying, which they believed would bring them closer to God. They followed the orders of the Pope in Rome, a link which Henry wanted to destroy. The monasteries also had big estates of farmland attached to them, and they often owned buildings and houses elsewhere. Henry wanted all this wealth for himself.

Modern monks - looking much the same now as in Henry VIII's time.

 Did you know?

The 80-year old Abbot of Glastonbury, in Somerset, refused to hand the abbey over to the King's men. For this, he was dragged up Glastonbury Tor (hill), hanged, drawn and quartered. His head was hung over the Abbey gates.

Glastonbury Abbey ruins

 Go and visit

Visit the ruined abbey in Glastonbury, Somerset (above), once the scene of violence when Henry VIII's men came to dissolve it. You can visit the ruins of many other abbeys that were suppressed at the Dissolution, for example, Fountains Abbey in Yorkshire.

The Dissolution

The destruction of the monasteries by Henry VIII is called the Dissolution. Cromwell sent troops to the monasteries, demanding that the monks close them down. Anyone who resisted was imprisoned and sometimes tortured or even executed. Cromwell accused monks of living drunken immoral lives, charges which were likely to have been at least partly made up.

The wealth goes to Henry

Once he had taken possession of the monasteries, Henry distributed many of them to his loyal followers. They took over farmland and, in some cases, monasteries were converted into houses. Others were left to crumble, having been stripped of their treasures. Stones from the buildings were sometimes used for new houses.

Key fact

There were about 850 monasteries in England before the Dissolution, providing homes for around 9,000 monks and nuns. They were all destroyed during the years 1536-40. Most of their inhabitants were simply thrown onto the street.

Prepared for war

The Pope was now Henry's sworn enemy. He declared Henry an enemy of the Roman Catholic Church and was willing to help anyone who would restore Papal power in England.

Henry was "excommunicated" which meant he was banned from the Church and therefore banned from heaven, according to Catholic belief.

Under threat
The country was now in constant fear of an invasion, and it was rumoured that both the Catholic Spanish and French kings were raising armies to invade England. The Scots invaded in 1542, with French support, but they were defeated at Solway Moss by the English. Meanwhile, Henry built forts and castles along the south coast, in case of an attack from the sea.

A south coast fort built by Henry to defend England from invasion.

Tudor soldiers

Ordinary soldiers in Henry's time did not wear much armour, only a helmet and a breastplate. They were expected to provide their own weapons. Muskets and pistols now appeared on battlefields because soldiers began to use gunpowder widely for the first time. They were also armed with pikestaffs, long wooden poles topped with spearpoints, or axes.

Henry's navy

Henry ordered that many new ships be built for his navy. He encouraged his gunmakers to come up with bigger, more powerful guns to smash through the sides of enemy ships at sea. He was very proud of his new ships and the prestige they gave him. They were fast, easy to move around and had gunports (square windows) cut into the hull where cannons were positioned.

 Key fact

The pride of Henry's fleet was the *Mary Rose* (above). Henry travelled to Portsmouth to see his ship sail out against the French fleet in 1545. However, the ship had its lower gunports open and water flooded in. It sank before Henry's eyes. The wreck of the *Mary Rose*, brought up from the seabed in 1982 after 400 years, can be seen at Portsmouth Historic Dockyard.

 Did you know?

The remains of 200 men and boys were discovered on the wreck of the *Mary Rose*, along with many sailors' possessions, such as clothes, gaming dice and even a backgammon set.

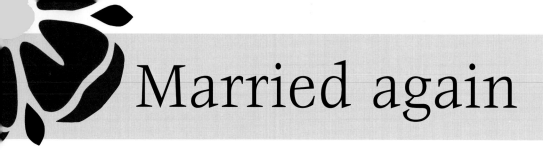

Married again

Henry is said to have been devastated by the death of Jane Seymour in 1537.

By 1540, he had still not remarried and his ministers were getting worried. England urgently needed a friendly alliance, through marriage, with another similar-thinking powerful country to help it against its Catholic enemies.

The best bride

Thomas Cromwell, Henry's chief minister, suggested an alliance with a German noble, the Duke of Cleves. Many Germans had also rejected the authority of the Roman Catholic Church and Cromwell thought they would make ideal political friends. He arranged for Henry to marry Anne, the Duke's sister.

A flattering portrait

Hans Holbein, Henry's court painter, was sent to paint a portrait of Anne. Henry admired the portrait, and agreed to marry Anne without meeting her. But Holbein had made her look prettier than she really was. When she arrived Henry thought she was very ugly, while she thought him monstrously fat and frightening. The marriage went ahead in January 1540 but divorce soon followed in July.

Portrait of
Anne of Cleves
by Hans Holbein

 Did you know?

After her divorce, Anne of Cleves was given the honorary title of "The King's Sister". She lived in England until her death, and was said to like English ale and gambling.

Cromwell falls

Henry blamed Thomas Cromwell for his disastrous marriage. Cromwell was arrested and executed, without even a trial. He had many enemies, who hated him for his part in splitting England from the Catholic Church. They did all they could to hasten his disgrace and death.

"I cry for mercy, mercy, mercy...," Cromwell wrote to Henry from his prison, but the King ignored his pleas.

 Key fact

It was a dangerous job being Henry's chief minister. It was easy to make enemies, who might seek revenge by persuading the King to turn against you in the future. By the time of Cromwell's death, Henry's court was no longer a carefree place but was full of distrust and fear.

 Go and visit

At the Tudor galleries of the National Portrait Gallery in London, you can come face-to-face with paintings of important figures in Henry's life including Henry himself, three wives, Wolsey, Cromwell and others.

 Portrait of Thomas Cromwell

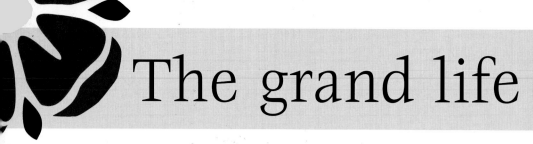

The grand life

Henry had several royal palaces. He lived in different ones at different times of the year, along with his court.

His palaces had to be big enough to house many people, and Henry was keen to impress foreign visitors with his wealth and power, so he spent a lot of money on building projects and on furnishings and luxuries.

Food aplenty

Coping with the King and his court was an enormous task, and the royal palaces needed many servants. There were huge kitchens to provide banquets for the entire court on a daily basis. Each day meat was roasted on spits over the kitchen fires. The menu might include wild boar, venison and even peacocks and swans. The Tudors also loved ornately decorated sweets made from almonds, dried fruit, spices and sugar.

Greenwich Palace, where Henry was born, faced on to the River Thames near London.

 Go and visit

Hampton Court has a huge Tudor kitchen (left), big enough for cooking the banquets Henry liked. Cotehele House in Cornwall also has a Tudor kitchen complete with the kinds of food that would have been cooked in Henry's time.

 Key fact

Henry saw his palaces as being symbols of his own power. That is why he made Thomas Wolsey hand over Hampton Court to him in 1528. Henry didn't like one of his ministers having a home grander than any of his own.

 Did you know?

Running water was piped into Hampton Court from a nearby spring, a very luxurious feature of the time. Most people had to go and collect water to use in their homes.

Smelly summer

Some of Henry's palaces were located on the River Thames outside London, in small villages such as Greenwich and Hampton (now built-up suburbs of London). The King and his court would sail by luxurious royal barge between the palaces. In summer, especially, they wished to avoid the centre of the city because of smell and disease brought on in hot weather.

Fires and furniture

The Tudor era saw a big rise in the attention to comfort and interior design inside the houses of wealthy people. Henry's palaces were decorated with intricate stone and plaster work, and comfortable upholstered furniture. Richly inlaid tapestries hung on the walls. Palaces such as Hampton Court had separate rooms, each with its own fireplace and chimneys to take away the smoke.

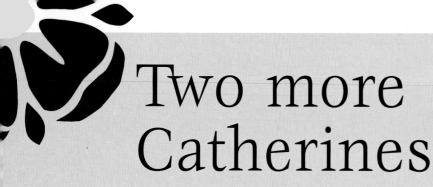

Two more Catherines

Henry married twice more before his death. His fifth wife was to prove as unlucky as the others. His sixth wife outlived him.

Catherine Howard was the niece of the Duke of Norfolk, an enemy of Thomas Cromwell. He saw the opportunity to get Henry to divorce Anne of Cleves, marry Catherine and hasten Cromwell's fall from power. Catherine was 19 and Henry was 49 when they married in 1540. She was soon accused of adultery, found guilty and beheaded, less than two years after the wedding. Unlike Anne Boleyn, it's thought she may well have been unfaithful to Henry.

Henry in his later years – a portrait painted in about 1537.

Did you know?

Catherine Howard asked for the executioner's block to be brought into her room the night before her execution, so she could practise putting her head on the block.

26

Go and visit

Sudely Castle, in Gloucestershire, where Catherine Parr lived after Henry's death. She got married again, to Thomas Seymour.

Wife number six

Henry married Catherine Parr, his sixth wife, in 1543. She had been married and widowed twice before. Catherine was a sensible influence and brought calm to Henry's later life. She had no children with Henry, but she encouraged Henry to take more interest in his daughters, Mary and Elizabeth, and she oversaw Prince Edward's education.

Henry married so many times during his life for different reasons: to produce an heir, to improve England's political standing and for love.

This stained glass window at Sudely Castle shows Catherine Parr and two of her husbands – Henry VIII and Thomas Seymour.

Key fact

Although Henry has become known as the king with six wives, he spent over twenty years married to just one of them, Catherine of Aragon. In the fourteen years from his first divorce to his death, he had five more wives.

The final years

Henry died at the age of 55 in January 1547. He was unrecognisable as the handsome, athletic young prince who had come to the throne.

Worsening health dogged him in his later years, and his temper became very unpredictable.

Stinking king

Henry was said to suffer from constant violent headaches which made him very bad-tempered. He developed poisonous ulcers on his legs and he could no longer walk. He smelled awful, and needed constant medical attention. His long-suffering sixth wife, Catherine Parr, nursed him through these difficult final years.

Dangerous old-age

As he aged, Henry became more suspicious of anyone who he thought might oppose him. By his order, many of his opponents were tortured and executed, some with good reason but some were innocent. His reign had begun with great happiness and hope, but by the end few people mourned his death.

Did you know?

Henry was so suspicious of others by the end of his reign, that he locked himself into his bedchamber at night, in case somebody tried to kill him.

A gigantic suit of armour made for Henry in his later years.

Trouble left behind

After Henry's death his frail nine-year old son Edward succeeded him, followed in turn by his two daughters, Mary and Elizabeth. Henry's break with the Roman Catholic Church caused violent trouble between Roman Catholics and Protestants in England throughout the reigns of his three children.

Key fact

Young Edward VI was a Protestant, who had Catholics put to death. His successor, Mary I, was a staunch Roman Catholic who put Protestants to death. Queen Elizabeth I, the last of the Tudor monarchs, was Protestant but she did not persecute people for their beliefs until later in her reign, when Roman Catholics plotted against her.

Portrait of Henry's son, Edward VI

Henry's tomb in St George's Chapel, Windsor Castle, next to the grave of Jane Seymour.

Go and visit

Henry's tomb in St George's Chapel, Windsor Castle, next to the grave of Jane Seymour. Several other English monarchs are also buried here.

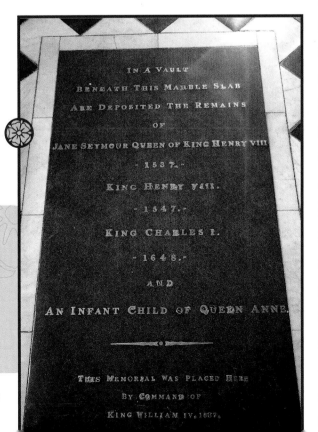

IN A VAULT
BENEATH THIS MARBLE SLAB
ARE DEPOSITED THE REMAINS
OF
JANE SEYMOUR QUEEN OF KING HENRY VIII
- 1537 -
KING HENRY VIII.
- 1547 -
KING CHARLES I.
- 1648 -
AND
AN INFANT CHILD OF QUEEN ANNE.

THIS MEMORIAL WAS PLACED HERE
BY COMMAND OF
KING WILLIAM IV. 1837.

GLOSSARY

alliance
A friendship between nations, particularly in wartime. Marriage between kings and queens of different nations was often used to make alliances.

anointing
Part of the coronation ceremony in which the new king or queen receives God's blessing.

annul
To declare officially that something never counted in the first place, such as Henry's marriage to Catherine of Aragon.

betrothal
An agreement between a man and a woman to marry. Catherine of Aragon was betrothed to Henry VIII.

Catholic Church
The Christian Church which has the Pope as its head.

civil war
War between two opposing sides from the same country.

coronation
The ceremony when the crown is placed on a new king or queen's head, to mark the official beginning of their reign.

Dissolution, the
The closing down and destruction of the monasteries in England and Wales, ordered by Henry VIII.

excommunication
The official exclusion of a person from the Catholic Church, supposed to condemn them to hell. The Pope did this to Henry.

heir
The next-in-line to the throne, generally the eldest son of the king.

jousting
An event in which knights tried to knock each other off their horses with lances.

noble
A member of the most powerful and wealthy families of the country, given titles such as Baron and Lord.

Pope
The head of the Catholic Church, based in Rome.

Protestant Church
A new branch of the Christian Church which was set up in Tudor times, rejecting the rule of the Pope.

reign
The period of a king or queen's rule.

tax
A sum of money that the people of a country are made to pay to the king's ministers, to raise money for the king to spend.

theology
The study of religion. Henry studied theology as a boy.

treason
The crime of plotting against a king or queen.

Tudor
The name of Henry VIII's family. Henry VII, Henry VIII, Edward VI, Mary I and Elizabeth I were all Tudor monarchs.

Tudor rose
The badge of the Tudor family, which combined a red and a white rose.

TIMELINE

1485 Henry Tudor defeats Richard III at the Battle of Bosworth Field, bringing an end to the Wars of the Roses. He is crowned King and the Tudor period begins.

1491 Prince Henry (later Henry VIII) is born at Greenwich Palace.

1502 Prince Arthur dies. Prince Henry becomes heir to the throne.

1509 Henry VII dies. Prince Henry marries Catherine of Aragon and is crowned King Henry VIII.

1513 The English army defeats the Scots at the Battle of Flodden.

1516 Princess Mary (later Mary I) born.

1533 Henry divorces Catherine of Aragon and marries Anne Boleyn.

1533 Princess Elizabeth (later Elizabeth I) born.

1533-34 The Act of Appeals and The Act of Supremacy are passed by Parliament, making the English Church independent of Rome and making Henry its head.

1536 Henry divorces Anne Boleyn and has her executed for treason. He marries Jane Seymour. The Dissolution of the monasteries begins.

1537 Prince Edward (later Edward VI) born.

1537 Jane Seymour dies.

1540 Henry marries, and divorces Anne of Cleves. Thomas Cromwell is executed. Henry marries Catherine Howard.

1542 Catherine Howard is executed.

1543 Henry marries Catherine Parr.

1545 The *Mary Rose* sinks.

1547 Death of Henry VIII.

WEBSITE SUGGESTIONS

www.royalarmouries.org
Find out about the Tudor weapons and armour at the National Museum of Arms and Armour.

www.maryrose.org
Find out about the *Mary Rose* exhibition. Take a virtual tour of the ship and meet the crew.

www.hrp.org.uk
The official site of both the Tower of London and Hampton Court. Click on the links to choose which one you'd like to find out about.

www.nationaltrust.org.uk
Find out about Tudor places to visit near you.

www.royalpaperdolls.com
Print off paper dolls of Henry and his wives, and find out all about them.